It's My State!

ALABAMA

The Yellowhammer State

Joyce Hart and Elissa Bass

Cavendish Square

New York

Published in 2016 by Cavendish Square Publishing, LLC
243 5th Avenue, Suite 136, New York, NY 10016

Copyright © 2016 by Cavendish Square Publishing, LLC

Third Edition

No part of this publication may be reproduced, stored in a retrieval system, or transmitted in any form or by any means—electronic, mechanical, photocopying, recording, or otherwise—without the prior permission of the copyright owner. Request for permission should be addressed to Permissions, Cavendish Square Publishing, 243 5th Avenue, Suite 136, New York, NY 10016. Tel (877) 980-4450; fax (877) 980-4454.

Website: cavendishsq.com

This publication represents the opinions and views of the author based on his or her personal experience, knowledge, and research. The information in this book serves as a general guide only. The author and publisher have used their best efforts in preparing this book and disclaim liability rising directly or indirectly from the use and application of this book.

CPSIA Compliance Information: Batch #CW16CSQ

All websites were available and accurate when this book was sent to press.

Library of Congress Cataloging-in-Publication Data

Hart, Joyce, 1954- author.
Alabama / Joyce Hart and Elissa Bass.
pages cm. — (It's my state!)
Includes index.
ISBN 978-1-62713-235-0 (hardcover) ISBN 978-1-62713-237-4 (ebook)
1. Alabama—Juvenile literature. I. Bass, Elissa. II. Title.
F326.3.H372 2014
976.1—dc23

2015023853

Editorial Director: David McNamara
Editor: Fletcher Doyle
Copy Editor: Rebecca Rohan
Art Director: Jeffrey Talbot
Designer: Alan Sliwinski
Senior Production Manager: Jennifer Ryder-Talbot
Production Editor: Renni Johnson
Photo Research: J8 Media

The photographs in this book are used by permission and through the courtesy of: Buyeniarge/Getty Images, cover; Susan Law Cain/Shutterstock.com, 4; Anatoliy Fyodorov/iStock/Thinkstock, 4; Maresa Pryor/Earth Scenes, 4; Josh Roswell/U.S. Fish and Wildlife Service/File:Alabama red-bellied turtle US FWS cropped.jpg/ Wikimedia Commons, 5; Istohnik/Shutterstock.com, 5; Tyler Boyes/Shutterstock.com, 5; Rob Hainer/Shutterstock.com, 6; Raymond Gehman/Corbis, 8; Heeb Christian/Prisma/agefotostock, 9; Tad Denson/Shutterstock.com, 12; Wire Eagle/Flickr, 14; Historic American Buildings Survey/File:Sixteenth Street Baptist Church section of the Milestone exhibition gallery in the Birmingham Civil Rights Institute.jpg/Wikimedia Commons, 14; loneroc/Shutterstock.com, 14; Danita Delimon/ Gallo Images/Getty Images, 15; Justin Sullivan/Getty Images, 15; James E Scarborough/Ke4roh/File:Apollo 16 capsule.JPG/Wikimedia Commons, 15; Warren Faidley/ Corbis, 16; Kevin Fleming/Corbis, 18; Buddy Mays/Corbis, 18; Stephen J. Krasemann, 20; Leonard Lee Rue III/Science Source/Getty images, 20; Michael P. Gadomski/ Photo Researchers, Inc., 20; Nancy Bauer/Shutterstock.com, 21; Ron Rowan Photography/Shutterstock.com, 21; Steve Oehlenschlager/Shutterstock.com, 21; Richard A. Cooke/Corbis, 22; North Wind Picture Archives, 24; De Agostini Picture Library/Getty Images, 25; Marilyn Angel Wynn/Nativestock/Getty Images, 26; DEA/G. Dagli Orti/Getty Images, 28; SuperStock, 31; North Wind Picture Archives, 32; North Wind Picture Archives, 33; Richard Cummins/SuperStock, 34; Danita Delimon/ Gallo Images/Getty Images, 34; Carol M. Highsmith/Buyenlarge/Getty Images, 35; Rob Hainer/Shutterstock.com, 35; Corbis, 36; Corbis, 37; Bettmann/Corbis, 38; Flip Schulke/Corbis, 39; Richard T. Nowitz/Corbis, 41; Rob Hainer/Shutterstock.com, 44; Carol M. Highsmith/Buyenlarge/Getty Images, 45; Focus on Sport/Getty Images, 48; Valery Marchive/File:Tim Cook 2009.jpg/Wikimedia Commons, 48; AP Photo/The Tuscaloosa News, Robert Sutton, 48; Reuters/Corbis, 49; Northfoto/Shutterstock. com, 49; Photo Works/Shutterstock.com, 49; Gary S Chapman/Getty Images, 51; Bettmannm, 53; TTstudio/Shutterstock.com, 54; Elzbieta Sekowska/Shutterstock. com, 54; AP Photo/Al.com, Bill Starling, 55; AP Photo/Dave Martin, 55; Nagel Photography / Shutterstock.com, 57; Heeb Christian/Prisma/agefotostock, 58; AP Photo/Dave Martin, 59; Richard Cummins/SuperStock, 60; Hulton Archive/Getty Images, 62; Michael Reynolds-Pool/Getty Images, 62; Matthew Cavanaugh/Getty Images, 62; Danita Delimon/Gallo Images/Getty Images, 64; U.S. Department of Agriculture/Photo Researchers, Inc., 66; Lowell Georgia/Corbis, 67; Paul Harcourt/ Shutterstock.com, 68; Mark Elias/Bloomberg via Getty Images, 68; M. E. Warren / Photo Researchers, Inc., 69; Philip Gould/Corbis, 69; Photosiber/Shutterstock.com, 70; Greg Smith/Corbis, 71; Danny E. Hooks/Shutterstock.com, 73; Christopher Santoro, 74; Stephen Saks/Lonely Planet Images/Getty Images, 75; Lonesome Crow/ File:Devil's Shoals.JPG/Wikimedia Commons, 75; Christopher Santoro (both), 76.

Printed in the United States of America

ALABAMA

CONTENTS

State Wildflower: Oakleaf Hydrangea

The oakleaf hydrangea was confirmed as Alabama's official state wildflower in 1999. Discovered by naturalist William Bartram as he traveled through the area between 1775 and 1776, it is native to all sixty-seven counties of the state. It can grow to 6 feet (1.8 meters) tall and produces beautiful white blooms in summer.

State Bird: Yellowhammer

One of the unofficial nicknames of Alabama comes from this bird. The yellowhammer is also called a flicker and is a member of the woodpecker family. The male yellowhammers have yellow feathers in their wings. Both males and females have sharp claws to help them cling to tree trunks.

State Tree: Southern Longleaf Pine

Officially named as the state tree in 1997, the southern longleaf pine grows in forests throughout the southern portions of Alabama. This pine tree has 12-inch (30.5-centimeter) needles that grow in clusters of three.

ALABAMA

⭐ State Animal: Alabama Red-Bellied Turtle

The Alabama red-bellied turtle is native to Alabama and lives in either fresh or brackish (somewhat salty) water in the Mobile Delta and in the waters of Baldwin County. This turtle lives in the wild only in Alabama. It was put on the US Fish and Wildlife Service's Endangered Species List in 1987.

⭐ State Nut: Pecan

Pecan trees thrive in Alabama, so it comes as no surprise that the pecan was named the state nut in 1982. It grows inside a thin, oval shell that is easy to crack. The sweet nut is a popular snack and is used in many Southern recipes.

⭐ State Rock: Marble

Alabama is known around the world for its marble, a rock made up of recrystallized limestone or dolomite. Marble comes in pink, red, gray, and black. Most of Alabama's marble is found in Talladega County from the Coosa River southward. Marble was designated the state rock in 1969.

The Little River has carved out a deep canyon on Lookout Mountain in the Cumberland Plateau in northeast Alabama. The area is part of the Little River Canyon National Preserve.

The Yellowhammer State

Alabama is located in the southeastern part of the United States. Its geography varies from forested mountains in the north to sandy beaches along the Gulf of Mexico in the south. With its gentle climate and friendly people, Alabama is a great place to live.

Alabama covers more than 52,000 square miles (134,679 square kilometers), making it the thirtieth-largest state. Alabama is almost rectangular, measuring about 300 miles (483 kilometers) north to south and about 200 miles (322 km) east to west. The land surface of the southern portion of the state is made up of low hills and flat valleys. As you travel from Mobile in the southwest to the Appalachian Mountains in the northeast, the elevation of the land slowly rises, changing from sea level to almost 2,000 feet (610 meters). If you completed a tour of the entire state, you would see everything from sandy shorelines to fertile valleys, broad prairies, swampy bogs, limestone caves, evergreen forests, and rocky mountainsides. Scientists have studied these features and have divided Alabama into six regions, each with its own distinctive traits.

The East Gulf Coastal Plain

The largest region is the East Gulf Coastal Plain, which covers most of the southern and western parts of Alabama. In the southern part of this plain is the Mobile River Delta,

Granite cliffs present a challenge to rock climbers in Cheaha State Park, near the highest point in the state.

Alabama Borders

North:	Tennessee
South:	Florida
	Gulf of Mexico
East:	Georgia
West:	Mississippi

where swamplands drain into the Gulf of Mexico. Alabama's major seaport is also located here.

In the northern part of the plain, which stretches almost to Tennessee, the land is creased with rows of hills that run in an east-to-west pattern. You will find farmlands and forests in this area. Farther east on the plain, cows, pigs, and poultry are raised. Peanut crops are also grown in the region. Large cities in this area include Mobile in the far south, Montgomery in the central portion, and Tuscaloosa farther north.

In the middle of the East Gulf Coastal Plain is the Black Belt, which runs along the Alabama River Valley. This strip of prairie land almost cuts the state in two, dividing northern and southern Alabama. This region got its name because of its black, sticky soil, which was, at one time, a great place to grow cotton. Today, farmers here mostly raise **livestock**. Selma is the region's major city.

The Piedmont Plateau

Northeast of the Black Belt region is the Piedmont **Plateau**. The highest point in Alabama, Mount Cheaha, which stretches to 2,408 feet (734 m), is located here in Lineville. Also found in the Piedmont Plateau are Alabama's famous marble quarries and other rock and mineral deposits, such as coal, iron, and limestone. The Piedmont Plateau is an area of hills, ridges, and valleys.

The Appalachian Ridge and Valley Region

Just north of the Piedmont is the Appalachian Ridge and Valley Region, where more deposits of coal, iron ore, and limestone are found. These minerals make up the ingredients for steel, which is produced in Alabama's steel mills. The southernmost tip of the Appalachian Mountains is located in this region. The Appalachian Mountains are a chain of mountains that run from Alabama to Maine.

The Cumberland Plateau

The Cumberland Plateau lies in the northeastern corner of Alabama. A plateau is an area of high ground that is level, such as a flattop mountain. Although the land in this area is relatively flat, in some places it still rises to about 1,800 feet (549 m).

The bodies of water in this area, such as Guntersville Lake, support almost one hundred different types of fish. There are many caves here, too, which are great habitats for different varieties of bats. Two of Alabama's most famous caves are in Cathedral Caverns State Park and Rickwood Caverns State Park.

There are many caverns in the Cumberland Plateau for people to explore.

ALABAMA
COUNTY MAP

ALABAMA
POPULATION BY COUNTY

County	Population	County	Population	County	Population
Autauga County	54,571	Dallas County	43,820	Marion County	30,776
Baldwin County	182,265	DeKalb County	71,109	Marshall County	93,019
Barbour County	27,457	Elmore County	79,303	Mobile County	412,992
Bibb County	22,915	Escambia County	38,319	Monroe County	23,068
Blount County	57,322	Etowah County	104,430	Montgomery County	229,363
Bullock County	10,914	Fayette County	17,241	Morgan County	119,490
Butler County	20,947	Franklin County	31,704	Perry County	10,591
Calhoun County	118,572	Geneva County	26,790	Pickens County	19,746
Chambers County	34,215	Greene County	9,045	Pike County	32,899
Cherokee County	25,989	Hale County	15,760	Randolph County	22,913
Chilton County	43,643	Henry County	17,302	Russell County	52,947
Choctaw County	13,859	Houston County	101,547	St. Clair County	83,593
Clarke County	25,833	Jackson County	53,227	Shelby County	195,085
Clay County	13,932	Jefferson County	658,466	Sumter County	13,763
Cleburne County	14,972	Lamar County	14,564	Talladega County	82,291
Coffee County	49,948	Lauderdale County	92,709	Tallapoosa County	41,616
Colbert County	54,428	Lawrence County	34,339	Tuscaloosa County	194,656
Conecuh County	13,228	Lee County	140,247	Walker County	67,023
Coosa County	11,539	Limestone County	82,782	Washington County	17,581
Covington County	37,765	Lowndes County	11,299	Wilcox County	11,670
Crenshaw County	13,906	Macon County	21,452	Winston County	24,484
Cullman County	80,406	Madison County	334,811		
Dale County	50,251	Marengo County	21,027		

Source: US Bureau of the Census, 2010

The Interior Low Plateau

The Interior Low Plateau lies in the northernmost part of the state. There the land is made up mostly of limestone, which is a whitish-colored rock usually made from the remains of ancient sea creatures. Fed by the Tennessee River, the fertile valleys in this section are ideal for farmers. Farms and ranches in the region raise cattle and other livestock and grow crops such as corn and cotton. Huntsville and Decatur are the biggest Alabama cities in this area.

The Waterways

Alabama has more than 900 square miles (2,331 sq km) of rivers and artificial, or manmade, lakes. There are twenty-six rivers in Alabama. The longest rivers are the Tombigbee River, which is 400 miles (644 km) long, and the Alabama River, which is 300 miles (483 km) long. Most of Alabama's major rivers run in a north-to-south direction and drain into the Gulf of Mexico. The one exception is the Tennessee River, which runs east to west. The Mobile, Alabama, and Tombigbee Rivers are three of the most important rivers in the state. The Alabama River flows from Montgomery and meets the Tombigbee to form the Mobile River just north of the city of Mobile.

There are no large naturally occurring lakes in Alabama. However, man-made dams on some of the state's rivers have created artificial lakes, such as Guntersville Lake on the Tennessee River. Damming of the Coosa River has formed Weiss, Lay, Mitchell, Jordan, and Logan Martin Lakes.

Mobile Bay is an estuary, where the Gulf of Mexico meets the many rivers that form the Mobile Delta.

"I grew up in Mobile, Alabama—somebody's got to be from Mobile, right?—and Mobile sits at the confluence of five rivers, forming this beautiful delta. And the delta has alligators crawling in and out of rivers filled with fish and cypress trees dripping with snakes, birds of every flavor."
—Mike deGruy, documentary filmmaker

At the southwestern tip of the state you can enjoy the warm waters of the Gulf of Mexico. Alabama's only outlet to the Gulf of Mexico is along Mobile Bay. The state's coastline along the Gulf is about 50 miles (80 km) long. When you add the coastlines that occur along Mobile Bay and other smaller inlets in the area, though, Alabama's shoreline measures more than 600 miles (966 km).

Mobile Bay is home to a unique natural occurrence called a jubilee, when many species of shrimp, crabs, and fish will spontaneously swarm near the water's edge along a particular stretch of shoreline. Scientists say this is an instinctive attempt to avoid temporary patches of oxygen-poor bay water, but the animals appear to be literally climbing or jumping out of the water. These jubilees usually happen at least once a year and offer a unique opportunity for recreational seafood harvesting along the eastern shore of the Bay.

Over the years, Alabama's beaches have been affected by erosion, which is the wearing away of land by wind and waves. In 2010, an offshore oil rig in the Gulf of Mexico exploded and sank. For almost three months, oil gushed into the Gulf, affecting Alabama's beaches and marine life.

The Climate

Alabamians enjoy a subtropical climate, which means they experience short, mild winters and long, warm summers. In winter, the average high temperature ranges between about 45 degrees Fahrenheit (7.2 degrees Celsius) and 55°F (12.7°C), depending on the elevation of the land. People living at higher elevations will have cooler weather than those living closer to sea level. During the summer, temperatures are usually closer to 85°F (29.4°C). Very low or very high temperatures are unusual. The highest temperature ever recorded in Alabama was 112°F (44.4°C) on September 5, 1925, in Centreville. The record low temperature was −27°F (−32.7°C) at New Market on January 30, 1966.

Thunderstorms are common in Alabama, especially in the southern parts of the state, where the warm air from the Gulf of Mexico mixes with the cooler air from the north.

Alabama Gulf Coast Zoo

Birmingham Civil Rights Institute

The Edmund Pettus Bridge

★1. Alabama Gulf Coast Zoo

This 16-acre (6.5-hectare) zoo in Gulf Shores has more than 250 exotic animals. An elevated observation deck allows unobstructed viewing. Lions, tigers, bears, tropical birds, reptiles and exotic felines are on display.

★2. Birmingham Civil Rights Institute

This state-of-the-art, multimedia facility houses exhibitions of historical events from post-World War I racial **segregation** to present-day racial progress. Since opening in 1992, the BCRI has been visited by more than two million people.

★3. DeSoto Caverns

This geologic marvel near Childersburg has a main room that is twelve stories high and longer than a football field. There is a sound, light, and water show on the cavern tour, and a park with more than twenty-five attractions.

★4. The Edmund Pettus Bridge

The Edmund Pettus Bridge, which spans the Alabama River in Selma, is one of the most iconic symbols of the **civil rights movement**. It serves as the starting point of the 54-mile (86.9 km) Selma to Montgomery National Historic Trail.

★5. Five Rivers: Alabama's Delta Resource Center

Located in Spanish Fort, the Center sits where the Mobile, Spanish, Tensaw, Apalachee and Blakeley Rivers flow into Mobile Bay. Its educational and recreational opportunities, including canoeing, hiking and wildlife tours, are spread over 250,000 acres (101,171 ha).

6. Fort Morgan State Historic Site

Fort Morgan was active during four wars—Civil, Spanish-American, and World Wars I and II. The 479-acre (194 ha) site includes military buildings, and a museum contains exhibits featuring historic artifacts.

7. Moundville Archeological Park

This mysterious site on the Black Warrior River was abandoned more than 550 years ago. It once was a city of about 300 acres (121 ha) where many people of the Mississippian Culture lived.

8. Rosa Parks Museum

This museum in Montgomery honors events that started the bus boycott and the early civil rights movement. It is built on the site of the old Empire Theatre, where Mrs. Parks made her historic stand in 1955.

9. Tannehill Ironworks Historical State Park

This park is spread over 1,500 acres (607 ha) in three counties near Birmingham. In the warmer months, a miller, a blacksmith, and other craftsmen demonstrate their skill in historic buildings. You can hike, camp, and ride a miniature train.

10. US Space and Rocket Center

This Huntsville facility is home to a Saturn V moon rocket. You can learn about the Space shuttle program and the International Space Station, and see artifacts from the space program, interactive exhibits, and space travel simulators.

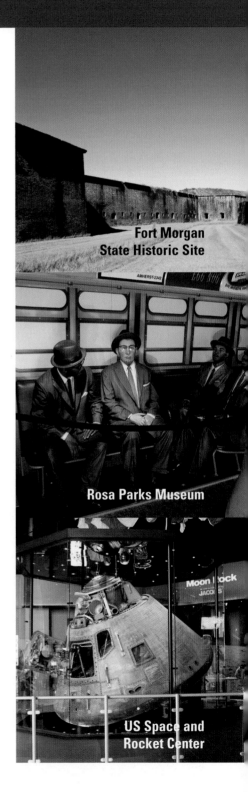

Fort Morgan State Historic Site

Rosa Parks Museum

US Space and Rocket Center

In the summer, Alabamians see a lot of rain, with rainfall ranges from 53 to 68 inches (135–173 centimeters) each year. Large storms such as hurricanes and tornadoes sometimes cross Alabama, causing flooding and very strong winds.

Sometimes snow falls in the winter, but usually only in the northern mountains. In March 1993, a storm crossed the state, causing as much as 20 inches (51 cm) of snow to fall over northern Alabama.

Natural Disasters

Alabama ranks fifth on the list of ten states in the country most likely to experience a natural disaster. Alabama has suffered $4.9 billion in property damage since 2007 and there have been 333 weather-related fatalities in the state. In April 2011, a series of tornadoes hit the Tuscaloosa and Birmingham areas, killing more than 120 people and injuring hundreds. Alabama is second only to Oklahoma in the number of EF5 tornadoes (the largest in intensity and area) that have struck there. The most frequent types of violent weather the state sees are thunderstorms, hail, and tornadoes.

The so-called Storm of the Century in 1993 dropped 13 inches (33 cm) of snow on Birmingham. During the Great Appalachian Storm of 1950, all-time record lows for November temperatures were set in Birmingham, 5°F (−15°C); Mobile, 22°F (−6°C); and Montgomery, 13°F (−11°C).

Hurricane Katrina in 2005 caused millions of dollars worth of damage to coastal areas of Alabama. The streets of Mobile were flooded by the storm's surge.

Amazingly Diverse Wildlife

Alabama ranks fourth in species diversity in the nation, after Hawaii, Florida, and California. Additionally, Alabama has the highest diversity for freshwater mussels, freshwater turtles, freshwater snails, and crayfish. Approximately 180 mussel species, or 60 percent of the nation's mussels, are found in Alabama, including several species that are found only in a specific locale in the state.

On Tuesday, April 29, 2003 at 3:59 a.m., Alabama was one of eleven states hit by a magnitude 4.6 earthquake. Its epicenter was 8 miles (13 km) east-northeast of Fort Payne. Damage was relatively minor and there were no deaths.

Wildlife

Alabama is home to a large number of different plants. Some of the most common trees include oak, hickory, magnolia, elm, ash, pine, and maple. There are trees that produce flowers, trees that are used for lumber, and trees that produce food. The most popular trees that produce nuts include the pecan and the black walnut. There are also trees that have medicinal qualities and are used to make people feel better. Sassafras is one example. Native Americans in the region made teas and liquid medicines from the roots of the tree.

Many different flowers grow in the state, but Alabama is most famous for its variety of azaleas. There are also several varieties of wildflowers, which you may see growing along the roadsides, in the prairies and mountains, and even in the backyards of many Alabamians.

Because Alabama has a lot of undisturbed or undeveloped land, there are many wild animals in the state. Raccoons, foxes, squirrels, deer, and rabbits can be found in Alabama's forests. There are also many larger animals, such as bobcats and bears. Beavers make their homes near Alabama's waterways.

Alabama's rivers, lakes, and streams are home to a variety of freshwater fish. These include bass, sunfish, pikes, eels, catfish, and perch. All of these fish provide food for Alabama's large wildlife, and they also attract human fishermen. It is not uncommon to see fishermen casting their lines in the early morning or early evening.

The state's coastal waters are also filled with aquatic life. Red snapper and grouper are types of fish that live on the coastal reefs. Other sea creatures, such as crabs, oysters, and shrimp, thrive in the Gulf's salty waters.

White egrets find plenty to eat in Alabama's marshes.

Many birds make their homes in Alabama. Some live there throughout the year, while others migrate to Alabama to stay warm during the winter. Birds in the Heart of **Dixie** include cardinals, wrens, bluebirds, yellowhammers, martins, hummingbirds, eagles, and hawks. Waterbirds such as ducks, loons, and herons can be found in or around the state's lakes and rivers. On the coast, Alabamians may see pelicans and cormorants. Because of the variety of birds in the state, Alabama is a favorite place for birdwatchers.

Alabama's Moon Trees

In 1971, Apollo 14's Command Module Pilot Stuart Roosa took tree seeds to the moon and back. Upon their return, the seeds were germinated and more than four hundred seedlings successfully grown. Most of the "moon trees" were given away in 1975 and 1976 to state forestry organizations, to be planted as part of the nation's bicentennial celebration. A loblolly pine seedling was presented to Governor George C. Wallace by the Alabama Forestry Commission and the US Forest Service in a special ceremony at the Governor's Office. The moon tree was planted on the lawn of the State Capitol as a "permanent reminder of man's flight into space and its relationship to the forests of America."

Protecting Alabama

As in other states, Alabama has many endangered and threatened plants and animals. Wildlife becomes threatened or endangered when habitats are lost, mostly through human interference such as cutting down forests or using land for buildings. Pollution also affects wild animal populations, either by directly harming the animals or hurting the food the animals eat. Government officials, scientists, and regular Alabama citizens are working hard to keep these animals from becoming extinct, or completely disappearing.

Alabama Power, a power company, maintains seven dams on the Coosa River. The dams provide electricity to many homes and businesses. They may also damage the wildlife that lives in and near the river.

One example of an endangered species in Alabama is the gray bat. Gray bats live in caves throughout Alabama, with the largest populations found in the northern part of

Endangered Species

Alabama lists 117 endangered or threatened species: 99 animals and 18 plants. It ranks third in the nation for the highest number of threatened and endangered species, behind Hawaii and California. It is estimated that nearly one hundred species have become extinct since colonial times. Nearly half of the endangered species on the list are types of mussels.

the state. The bats choose caves that are close to rivers or lakes because their diet is made up of insects that live on or near water. Cutting down trees around caves takes away the protective covering that gray bats need to fly safely to and from the water. In recent years, the loss of habitat has caused gray bats to be put on the Endangered Species list.

In the past, Alabama was not known for its environmental protection programs, but that has changed. Over time, Alabamians have become more informed about keeping the state's water clean and protecting all its wild creatures—right down to the tiny beach mouse.

Around the state, many organizations have been established to keep the natural beauty of Alabama alive. Groups of volunteers have come together to protect the state's wildflowers, the great rivers, the lush forests, and the coastal beaches. Alabamians are working hard. They know they live in a wonderful state, and they want to keep it that way.

A lake near Eufaula provides a safe habitat to an American alligator.

Black Bear

Eastern Spotted Skunk

Goldenrod

1. Alabama Canebrake Pitcher Plant

The Alabama canebrake pitcher plant is a carnivorous plant found only in central Alabama. It is shaped like a horizontal tube, and it produces nectar near the opening of the tube that attracts insects. The insects are trapped and digested by enzymes.

2. Black Bear

The black bear is the official state mammal of Alabama. Black bears usually stand between 4 and 7 feet (1.2–2.1 m) tall. Adult males can weigh as much as 500 pounds (227 kilograms). Black bears eat plants, berries, nuts, fruits, and insects.

3. Eastern Spotted Skunk

The Eastern spotted skunk is also called the civet cat or polecat. About the size of a squirrel, its black and white fur actually displays a distinctive striped pattern. When threatened, it does a handstand, arching its back while aiming its scent gland at the source of the threat.

4. Flattened Musk Turtle

This small freshwater turtle is found only in the Black Warrior River system in west-central Alabama. A bottom-dweller that is primarily nocturnal, it is listed as endangered because of a loss of habitat.

5. Goldenrod

Once the state flower, goldenrod is a common wildflower. All goldenrod plants have long spikes of bright yellow flowers. Goldenrods attract butterflies, and many Alabamians plant the flowers to attract these pretty insects.

6. Monarch Butterfly

The eastern tiger swallowtail is the state butterfly, but the monarch butterfly is the official insect. Monarchs have bright orange, black, and white wings, and lay their eggs on milkweed plants, which are found throughout the state.

Monarch Butterfly

White-Tailed Deer

Wild Turkey

7. Poison Ivy

Poison ivy berries are the yellowhammer's favorite food. The plant's oils can cause painful and very itchy skin problems. Poison ivy's glossy, three-leafed form makes it easy to identify.

8. Red Hills Salamander

This salamander is found only in the Red Hills district (Tallahatta and Hatchetigbee geologic formations) of south-central Alabama, where it burrows into the siltstone. This salamander is the official state amphibian.

9. White-Tailed Deer

White-tailed deer are found all over Alabama. As fawns, they have white spots on their sides. As they grow, the spots disappear and their coats turn mostly brown. The deer's keen senses of smell and hearing help to keep it out of danger.

10. Wild Turkey

The wild turkey population in Alabama was once low. Through conservation, they are back. Wild turkeys can grow to be 4 feet (1.2 m) long from head to tail. They are fast fliers, especially over short distances. They can sometimes go as fast as 55 miles per hour (89 kmh).

Moundville Park contains sites long abandoned by a Native American group known as the Mound Builders. The area is south of what is now Tuscaloosa.

From the Beginning

The first people to live in the land now known as Alabama are often called Paleo-Indians. Paleo means older or ancient. Scientists have estimated these early inhabitants may have lived here as many as nine thousand years ago. It is believed they originally came from Asia to North America across a land bridge between the two continents that no longer exists.

Paleo-Indians may have first reached the region that includes Alabama around 7000 BCE. They made homes in the many limestone caves. The caves sheltered them from the rain and the cold in winter and kept them cool in summer. The thick forests and clear rivers provided them with food. They hunted bear and deer, gathered nuts and fruits, and caught fish and turtles.

Paleo-Indians used stones to make arrowheads, scrapers, and drills. They used animal bones to make fish hooks and other tools.

Several thousand years later, the native people living in the region built large mounds. Scientists and historians today often call these people Mound Builders. Some native groups built homes on top of the mounds. Other groups built religious temples or used the mounds as sacred burial places. The Mound Builders disappeared after living in the area for about six hundred years. No one knows what happened to them. They may have been wiped out by disease.

It is also possible that they ran out of food and moved to another region. Some of the mounds remain in many states. In Alabama, mounds still exist in Hale County and Baldwin County, and on Dauphin Island.

The Creek Confederacy

Many years after the Mound Builders disappeared, new groups of native people began living in the region. Although these bands of natives each had their own names, the British later referred to them as Creeks. This was because the natives built their villages on the banks of creeks, or small branches of larger rivers.

> ### In Their Own Words
>
> "Maycomb was an old town, but it was a tired old town when I first knew it. ... There was no hurry, for there was nowhere to go, nothing to buy and no money to buy it with, nothing to see outside the boundaries of Maycomb County."
> –Scout Finch in *To Kill A Mockingbird* by Harper Lee

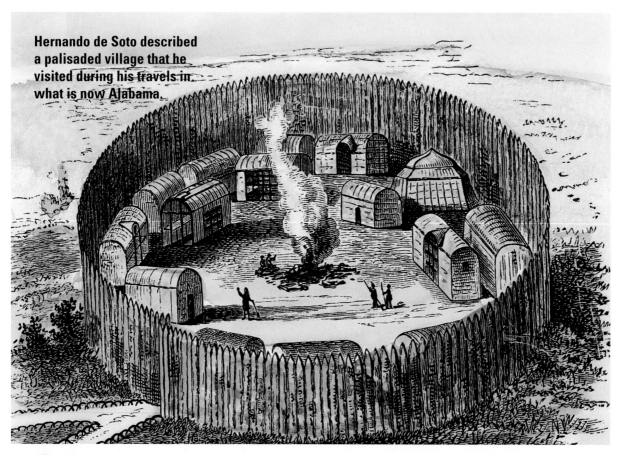

Hernando de Soto described a palisaded village that he visited during his travels in what is now Alabama.

This 1853 painting by William Henry Powell depicts Hernando de Soto discovering the Mississippi River near Natchez in 1541. The explorer was the first European to come across the river.

When Europeans arrived in the Creeks' land, the Creeks formed a larger group, called the Creek Confederacy, to protect themselves. The Confederacy was made up of more than seventeen native groups that spoke the same language, which was called Muskogean.

The Creeks were farmers. They grew corn, beans, and squash and raised cows, pigs, and horses. They lived in well-organized villages. Each community had its own leaders who met every day to discuss problems and solutions.

The Creeks enjoyed having fun. One of their favorite activities was a game called chunkey. Stones were rolled across the ground, and then spears were thrown as close to the stones as possible. Foot races were another popular activity.

Although the Creeks fought with the earliest European explorers, they learned to trust later settlers and even offered food to prevent these Europeans from starving. The Creeks were very generous. They welcomed strangers to their villages and eventually adjusted to many of the European customs. Many Creeks even married Europeans.

The Spanish Explorers

Europeans explored the coastline of present-day Alabama as early as the sixteenth century, but no one is certain of the exact date. Historians do know that the outline of Mobile Bay first appeared on a map of North America in 1505. It was not until 1519, however, that an official

The Native People

When European explorers first arrived in the region that is now called Alabama, the area was home to seven major tribes, Alabama, Biloxi, Cherokee, Chickasaw, Choctaw, Koasati, and Muskogee. The Muskogee was a strong union of tribes grouped into tribal towns, including the Abihka, Coosa, and Tallapoosa. The name Alabama came from the Muskogee word for "campsite" or "clearing." It is believed that at least three of the tribes, the Muskogee, Choctaw, and Chickasaw, had migrated north from Mexico, fleeing the explorer Cortez.

A Creek man wearing traditional clothing dances at a powwow.

Native people inhabited the area known as Alabama dating back nine thousand years, and while there were wars among some of the tribes, for the most part each tribe lived life in its territory. The Cherokee remained largely separate, with a distinct language, while other tribes shared attributes and some language. The Chickasaws were hunters and feared warriors, while the Choctaws were more agricultural.

The first European explorers to meet Alabama's native people were Spanish, sometime around 1528. The first documented encounter was with Spanish explorer Hernando de Soto in 1539. But the English and the French were not far behind, and soon the region was host to all three European nationalities. All of them were vying for trade with and dominance over the native people. The Spanish, English and French all had active relationships with different tribes between the 1690s and the 1750s, which is when the French and Indian War broke out. The French established the first permanent European settlement in Alabama at Fort Louis de la Mobile in 1702. Most Native Americans were forced to leave Alabama during the Indian Removals of the 1800s, sent to reservations in Oklahoma and Texas.

Today, the state of Alabama has one federally recognized tribe, and a number of state-recognized tribes. In 1984, the Alabama Indian Affairs Commission (AIAC) was created to represent more than thirty-eight thousand Native American families who are residents of the State of Alabama. The federally recognized tribe is of Creek descent, called Poarch Creek, and its reservation is near the town of Atmore. Unlike many other native tribes, the Poarch Creeks were not removed from their tribal lands and have lived together for almost two hundred years in and around the reservation in Poarch.

Spotlight on the the Poarch Band of Creek Indians

The Poarch Band of Creek Indians are descendants of a segment of the original Creek Nation, which once covered almost all of Alabama and Georgia. There are two Creek tribes today, the Poarch Creeks in Alabama and the Oklahoma Creeks.

Distribution: The Poarch Creeks in Alabama live on a reservation, located 8 miles (13 km) northwest of Atmore, which is land that belongs to the tribe and is under their control. The tribe has about 2,340 members, and of those tribal members, about 1,000 live on or near the 230-acre (93 hectare) reservation.

Homes: The Creek people lived in villages of single-family houses arranged around a village square. Creek houses were made of plaster and river cane walls with thatched roofs, typical of most native homes of that region. Often the houses were round.

Food: In Creek society, the men hunted and the women did the farming. They grew corn, beans, and squash. Homes had stone hearths, and their food included soups and stews.

Clothing: Creek men wore breechcloths or leggings, and women wore wraparound skirts and mantles made of woven cloth or deerskin. They all wore moccasins. Creek men had elaborate tattoos and used face paint for rituals, but the women did not decorate their skin.

Art: The Creeks were known for—and traded—their baskets, wood carvings, and glazed pottery, as well as beadwork.

René-Robert Cavelier, Sieur de La Salle, claimed the area that includes Alabama for France. He was killed by his own men in Texas.

visit was recorded: Spain's Alonso Álvarez de Pineda sailed into Mobile Bay but did not stay there very long.

In 1539, Hernando de Soto, the governor of Cuba, landed in what is now Tampa Bay, Florida. He had with him a well-armed group of about seven hundred men. First, de Soto marched his men to what is now Tennessee, and then turned south and entered the area of present-day Alabama. De Soto was looking for gold. When he could not find it, he went into Native American villages, forced his way into their homes, and stole anything of value. De Soto and his men also often beat and tortured the native people if they did not follow his orders. His men also stole their food. Word of Hernando de Soto's bad reputation began to spread throughout the different native groups, and eventually the natives decided to fight back.

In October 1540, a chief named Tuscaloosa planned a surprise attack on de Soto's army. The battle at Mabila did not go well for Tuscaloosa's men. Most of them were killed, as were many soldiers in de Soto's army. Although de Soto won this battle, he decided to leave the area because his surviving soldiers were badly wounded.

It would take almost twenty years before another group of Spanish explorers entered the region. Don Tristán de Luna y Arellano came with settlers who tried to establish a colony near Mobile Bay. Luna was also looking for gold. Like de Soto before him, Luna did not find it. Many of his people died from disease or hunger. After three years, the Spanish colony was abandoned.

The French Colonists

In 1689, the explorer René-Robert Cavelier, often called Sieur de La Salle, traveled down the Mississippi River and claimed for France all the land around it. This included present-day Alabama. He named the land the Louisiana Territory. Ten years later, in 1699, two brothers, Pierre and Jean-Baptiste Le Moyne, landed on Dauphin Island in Mobile Bay, ready to take on their jobs as governors of the territory.

By 1702, the first permanent European settlement in Alabama was established at the mouth of Mobile Bay. Life there was not easy. There was very little food and many diseases. There were also constant battles with pirates and Spanish settlers who still lingered in the area.

These early French settlers tried hard to raise crops, but they found that they needed a lot more help with the labor. They brought over about six hundred **slaves**—the first black slaves to enter the region. Even this extra help did not save the settlers, though. The French might have starved to death had the Creeks not shared their food with them.

The French finally found they could make more money selling furs from wild animals, such as beavers. With British fur trappers moving into the area, the competition for the land and the fur trade grew very serious. The dispute over who had the right to hunt on the land erupted into what would be called the French and Indian War. Many Native Americans sided with the French as they fought the British. The French were defeated, though, and had to sign the Treaty of Paris of 1763. This forced the French to surrender all their land east of the Mississippi River, which included present-day Alabama. The British now controlled the region.

Statehood

After winning the French and Indian War, the British controlled the area of Alabama for fewer than twenty years. In the late 1770s, the British colonies on the Atlantic Coast went to war for their independence from Great Britain. The colonists won the Revolutionary War and the new government signed another Treaty of Paris in 1783. The victory over Great Britain gave the newly formed United States the right to the land east of the Mississippi River. Spain argued against this claim, stating that it still owned the southern coastline around Mobile. The United States did not have full control over the region. It was not until the end of the War of 1812 (fought between Great Britain and the United States) that the United States government finally gained control of all the land that today includes Alabama.

In 1817, the land was named the Territory of Alabama. Two years after that, Alabama become a state. Alabama was fully admitted to the United States on December 14, 1819. The new state's legislators, or lawmakers, first met in Huntsville. Cahaba was the next city to serve as Alabama's capital, until 1826, when Tuscaloosa was chosen. Montgomery was voted as the new state capital in 1846, and it is Alabama's capital city today.

Making an Alabama Red-Bellied Turtle

You can make your very own family of Alabama red-bellied turtles just by changing the size of the circle cut from the construction paper.

What You Need

Red or orange construction paper
Yarn (green or multicolored)
Glue
Green pipe cleaner
Googly eyes

What To Do

- Cut a 2-inch (5 cm) circle from construction paper. The circle can be larger if you wish to make an adult turtle. You can make yours as big as you'd like. Cut a smaller circle for the head.

- Spread glue around your circle.

- Starting in the center of your circle start winding the yarn in a flat spiral. Try to make your spiral as tight as you can.

- Continue the spiral all the way to the edge of the paper circle, adding more glue as you go if necessary. Cut the yarn and glue the end in place.

- Cut some green pipe cleaner and make some small U-shaped legs for your turtle, as well as a tail. Turn your "shell" over and glue the turtle's parts onto the back. Glue on your googly eyes and you're done!

Andrew Dexter was among the founders of Montgomery.

By the 1850s, Alabama's economy was booming, mostly because of cotton. People from all over the states came to Alabama, and many brought hundreds of slaves with them. This brought prosperity to Alabama, but it also brought problems.

As more settlers and farmers arrived, pressure was put on the native groups to give up their land. Unfair treaties between the United States and Native Americans were written. Native Americans were often forced to sign the treaties, and in many cases, the United States did not keep their promises.

In 1830, US president Andrew Jackson signed the Indian Removal Act. The law let the US government negotiate with Native Americans and move them to federal territory west of the Mississippi in exchange for the Native Americans signing over their land in already established states.

Some of the tribes negotiated peacefully but others resisted and were forcibly removed. Most of the Native Americans who had once lived in Alabama were forced to move. Among them were the Cherokee. In the fall and winter of 1838–1839, the Cherokee were moved to Oklahoma in one of the most famous forced removals of Native Americans, called the Trail of Tears. Tens of thousands of Native Americans were forced to march west for more than 1,000 miles (1,609 km). During the march, almost four thousand Native Americans died from cold, hunger, or disease.

Most of the Cherokee lived in Georgia, but some came from northeastern Alabama. The Cherokee were rounded up at collection stockades for the march. They only facility in Alabama used for this purpose was Fort Payne in DeKalb County. Fort Payne was built in 1838 to hold the Native Americans before the march.

Civil War and Reconstruction

By 1860, Alabama was producing a record amount of cotton. In order to handle all the labor, Alabama's farmers bought thousands of slaves. So many slaves lived in the state during this time that Alabama's black population almost equaled its white population.

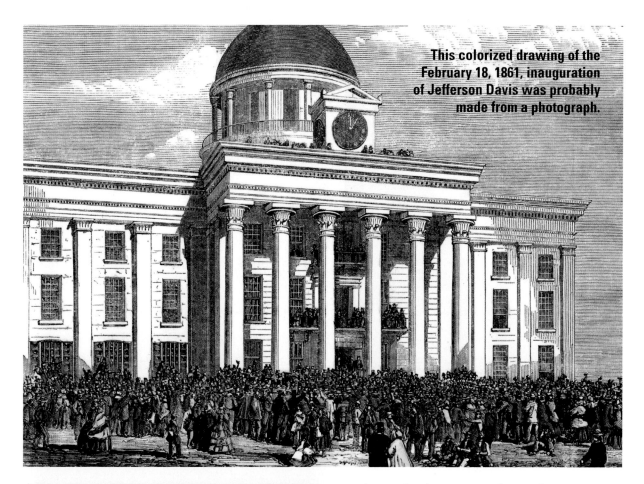

This colorized drawing of the February 18, 1861, inauguration of Jefferson Davis was probably made from a photograph.

President of the Confederacy

Jefferson Davis was sworn in as President of the Confederate States of America in Montgomery on February 18, 1861. Nine days earlier, a constitutional convention had met in the city and considered Davis and Robert Toombs of Georgia. Davis had widespread support from six of the seven states and easily won.

When Abraham Lincoln—who opposed slavery—was elected president, many people in Alabama and other Southern states were upset. Part of the reason was because they did not want to lose their slaves. Slave labor was necessary for Southern plantations to be successful. Southern states made plans to secede, or break away, from the United States.

In 1861, leaders from the Southern states met in Montgomery and created a new nation called the Confederate States of America. Montgomery was the Confederacy's capital. Jefferson Davis, former US Senator from Mississippi, was elected provisional president of the Confederacy. Two months later, war broke out between Confederate soldiers and Union, or Northern, forces. Not all Alabamians favored the

Confederacy. Some Alabamians did not believe in slavery. These people either hid in the northern hills of Alabama, refusing to fight, or they joined the Union army. Also, many slaves managed to run away, and some of them also joined the Northern forces.

There were no major battles fought on Alabama's soil. However, Union forces occupied several Alabama cities. Many Alabamians' lives were lost during the Civil War. There was a big battle in Mobile Bay because it was an important port through which the Confederate forces received supplies. The Union knew it had to take control of this port, so its troops fought the Confederate forces and won in 1864. A year later, the Civil War ended when the South surrendered.

Alabama does not have an official state nickname, but two unofficial ones refer back to the Civil War. The Yellowhammer State nickname began during the war. Its origin is either the yellow tinge in the gray "home-dyed" Confederate uniforms or the yellow trim on those uniforms. The soldiers who wore these uniforms looked like the yellowhammer, the state bird, which has yellow feathers on its wings. The nickname "Heart of Dixie" reflects the central role that Alabama played in the history of the South, including Montgomery's role as the first Confederate Capital. The Cotton State was also once in use because of the importance of the crop to the economy, but this was true of other Southern states.

The Union gained control of the port in Mobile in 1864 by winning the Battle of Mobile Bay.

10 KEY CITIES ★ ★ ★

Birmingham

Tuscaloosa

1. Birmingham: population 212,237

Named for Birmingham, England, in the days of post–Civil War Reconstruction, this city was founded in 1871. Through the end of the 1960s, it was a primary industrial center of the South.

2. Montgomery: population 205,764

The capital of Alabama is named for Richard Montgomery, an Irish-born soldier who served as a Major General in the Continental Army during the Revolutionary War. The first White House of the Confederacy and a Civil Rights Museum honoring forty-one people who died in the struggle are located here.

3. Mobile: population 195,111

Located at the head of Mobile Bay, the Port of Mobile is key to the city's economy dating back to trading between the French and Native Americans. Today it is the twelfth-largest port in the United States.

4. Huntsville: population 180,105

"The Rocket City" has the highest per capita income in the Southeast. Scientists were first attracted when the United States built a chemical munitions plant there. Now it is home to NASA's US Space and Rocket Center.

5. Tuscaloosa: population 90,468

Tuscaloosa is home to the University of Alabama, the state's largest university. It opened in 1831. Stillman College, which opened in 1875, is a historically black liberal arts college. It is also located in Tuscaloosa, as is Shelton State Community College.

6. Hoover: population 81,619

The largest suburb of Birmingham sits above the Cahaba Coal Fields, which spurred the city's development. It was home for more than twenty years to the Barons Minor League Baseball team, which returned to Birmingham in 2013.

7. Dothan: population 65,496

Dothan is called "The Peanut Capital of the World" because about one-fourth of the US peanut crop is produced nearby. Much of the crop is processed in plants located in the city.

8. Decatur: population 55,683

During the Civil War, the Union army occupied the city, and a general ordered all but four buildings destroyed. The four buildings are still standing: Old State Bank, Dancy-Polk House, Todd House, and the Burleson-Hinds-McEntire House.

9. Auburn: population 53,380

US News placed Auburn on its list of ten best places to live in the US in 2009. The city's unofficial nickname is "The Loveliest Village On The Plains," taken from the poem "The Deserted Village" by Oliver Goldsmith.

10. Madison: population 42,938

Madison was the site of a battle in the Civil War on May 17, 1864, when Confederate troops drove out Union infantry. Since 1990, the city's population has nearly tripled, growing along with nearby Huntsville.

Dothan

Auburn

Life was not easy after the Civil War for either white or black people in the South. The Jim Crow laws limited the legal rights of African Americans. The laws prevented many blacks from voting or holding public office. They also led to public schools, restaurants, bathrooms, and many other places being segregated, or separated by race. There was a shortage of food and farms, crops had been destroyed, and there were not many jobs available. Even though freed slaves enjoyed privileges they had never been given before, they did not enjoy them for very long. The Alabama government had signed the Fourteenth Amendment to the US Constitution, which guaranteed equal protection under the law to all citizens, including freed slaves. However, Alabama created its own state laws that took away many rights from African Americans. **Reconstruction**, the name given to the

Alabama, at Sea

At least seven United States Navy vessels have been named after Alabama. They include a storeship in 1819, a troop transporter in 1849, a merchant vessel in 1861, a pre-dreadnought battleship in 1900, a motorboat in 1917, a battleship in 1942, and a submarine that is currently still in service.

Mill workers, including children, turned cotton into material for clothing, blankets, and other goods.

Workers of all ages kept the mines open to assist in the war effort in the early 1900s.

rebuilding of the South, helped Alabama recover from the war. Life in Alabama was slowly improving, but not all of Alabama's citizens were benefiting from these changes.

Changing Times

Farming continued to be a major source of income for many Alabamians at the end of the 1800s. The processing of iron in northeastern Alabama created new jobs and a new city. Birmingham, located in the heart of the mining lands, was founded in 1871.

Another important industry at this time was cotton textiles. Cotton textiles were used to make things like sheets, clothing, and towels. Railroads, which had been built during Reconstruction, helped Alabama's industries by providing transportation for goods. The products were taken from the factories to other cities or to Mobile Bay, where they were shipped out of the state.

During the first half of the twentieth century, an insect called the **boll weevil** destroyed much of Alabama's cotton crop. New food crops, such as peanuts, were planted. This helped to save many people from having to close down their farms. Alabama's economy was also helped when the United States entered World War I. American factories and farms produced supplies that the troops needed during the war.

In 1929, however, the American economy took a downward turn. The Great Depression hit the country and many stores and banks went out of business. Many Americans lost their jobs. Farms failed and had to be closed. Employment in Birmingham dropped from one hundred thousand full-time jobs to only fifteen thousand. Some people believe the Great Depression affected Birmingham more than any other city in the United States. Many Alabamians left the state to look for jobs. The US government did what it could to help the people, establishing work programs throughout the country. Under these programs, laborers built and repaired roads and bridges, or worked in lumber mills in the nation's forests.

The United States entered World War II in 1941, and this helped the country's economy. Factories and farms again had to provide needed supplies for American troops. Several states' economies, including Alabama's, improved.

In the 1950s, a new industry brought more jobs and prosperity to parts of Alabama. Huntsville became an important center for rocket and space research. The Saturn V rocket was developed at NASA's (National Aeronautics and Space Administration's) Space Flight Center in Huntsville. In 1969, a Saturn V rocket propelled *Apollo 11* into space. It carried Neil Armstrong, who became the first man to walk on the moon.

Rosa Parks started a chain of events that changed the United States when she refused to give up her seat on a Montgomery bus.

Around the time the space program was developing, African Americans began fighting for their civil rights. They had grown tired of being denied the rights granted to white citizens. They fought against segregation, which was a system that separated whites from blacks. Because of segregation, African Americans could not shop at some stores, could not eat at certain restaurants, and had to sit in the backs of public buses. Many African Americans could only hold low-paying jobs because they were not given better opportunities. Black children could not attend the same schools as white children, and the all-black schools were not given enough government money and did not have the same programs or supplies as schools for white children. In many cases, African Americans in parts of the United States were still not allowed to vote.

The civil rights movement, in which many African Americans and whites led peaceful marches and protests, was very active in Alabama. In 1955,

Vivian Malone

In 1963, Vivian Malone was one of two black students to enroll at the University of Alabama, defying the governor. On May 30, 1965, she became the first black person to graduate from the University of Alabama in its 134 years, with a degree in business management.

Dr. Martin Luther King Jr. *(center)* and his wife Coretta Scott King led a march in support of voting rights through the streets of Selma in March 1965.

The Birmingham Campaign

The Rev. Dr. Martin Luther King Jr. helped organize the Birmingham campaign in 1963 to bring attention to African-American integration efforts. The Birmingham campaign was a model of nonviolent protest and drew the world's attention to racial segregation in the South. It paved the way for the Civil Rights Act of 1964.

Rosa Parks refused to give up her seat on a Montgomery city bus to a white man. She was arrested for this, which led to the Montgomery bus boycott.

"I knew someone had to take the first step, and I made up my mind not to move," the brave Parks said.

During the boycott, Alabama citizens—black and white—who opposed segregation refused to use Montgomery's buses. In 1956, the United States Supreme Court—the highest court in the country—declared segregated bus seating illegal. This marked the beginning of the civil rights movement.

The Rev. Dr. Martin Luther King Jr., a pastor of a church in Montgomery, brought the hardships of everyday life of blacks to the attention of people throughout the United States and the world. He stood up for African Americans after the arrest of Parks. He advocated **desegregation**.

"And we are determined here in Montgomery to work and fight until justice runs down like water, and righteousness like a mighty stream," Dr. King wrote on December 5, 1955.

In 1965, Dr. King organized three Alabama marches in the fight for civil rights. They began in Selma and ended in Montgomery, 54 miles (87 km) away. The people in these marches were fighting for African Americans' right to vote. It would be a long, hard battle, but eventually African Americans would gain their equal rights.

The marches were based in Selma because of an active campaign in that city to allow blacks to vote. A group called the Dallas County Voters League (DCVL) launched a voter registration campaign in Selma in 1963, but after two years it had made no gains, even after the Civil Rights Act of 1964 ended legal segregation. In January 1965, the DCLV invited Dr. King and other prominent civil rights leaders to Selma. Thousands of people were being arrested in Selma during protests. The first march was planned after activist and deacon Jimmie Lee Jackson died on February 26, 1965. He had been shot by a state trooper during a peaceful protest in Marion, Alabama.

The first march took place on March 7, 1965. State troopers and local police attacked the unarmed marchers with billy clubs and tear gas after they passed over the county line, and the day became known as Bloody Sunday. The second march took place March 9 but never even made it off the bridge, and that night a group of white people beat to death a white minister from Boston named James Reeb. He had answered a call Dr. King made to clergy to come to Selma to protest the violence. The subsequent uproar in Alabama and across the nation led President Lyndon Johnson to introduce the Voting Rights Act to Congress.

The third march started March 21 under the protection of thousands of US soldiers and the Alabama National Guard. The marchers arrived in Montgomery on March 24 and reached the Alabama State Capitol on March 25. More than twenty-five thousand people were part of the march at the finish. The route is memorialized as the "Selma To Montgomery Voting Rights Trail," and is designated as a US National Historic Trail.

In 2014, a film called *Selma* was released. It was directed by Ava DuVernay and written by Paul Webb. *Selma* received four Golden Globe Award nominations, including Best Motion Picture—Drama, Best Director, and Best Actor, and won for Best Original Song. It received two Academy Award nominations, for Best Picture and for Best Original Song, winning the latter.

Young people get hands-on experience at the United States Space Camp in Huntsville.

Modern Alabama

From the end of the twentieth century and into the first decades of the twenty-first century, Alabama has undergone some changes. The population increased and new residents began living in different parts of the state. In the early 1900s, most Alabamians lived in rural communities and held jobs related to farming and agriculture. During the last half of the century, though, more than 60 percent of the population moved to the cities or the areas right outside the cities. This was a major shift for Alabama, which had previously been a very rural state. From 1970 on, people were moving away from farms in increasing numbers. They settled in the cities to

Heart of the Space Program

The George C. Marshall Space Flight Center [MSFC] in Huntsville has been a key facility in the American space program since its inception in 1960. The center provided the rockets that took the first man to the moon in 1969, developed the first space station [Skylab, 1973 to 1979], and has been an integral part of the programs that oversee the Hubble Space Telescope and the Shuttle Program.

find nonagricultural jobs, such as those in manufacturing and social services.

This caused an increase in suburban areas around Alabama's larger cities. Many counties around Alabama's cities doubled in population. Counties with a more rural setting lost half or more of the people who used to live there. Instead of being spread out throughout the state, people were living in clusters in urban areas. While this was good for the cities' economies, this also meant that problems such as air pollution, traffic jams, and school crowding became worse. Meanwhile, poverty increased in the rural areas as the loss of population forced stores and businesses to close.

Today, people are searching for solutions to help the rural counties find ways to make money and to keep Alabama's cities clean and safe. Officials are trying to attract new industries to provide more jobs, both in urban and rural areas. Other people are focusing on how to adjust to the swiftly growing cities.

Although the twenty-first century is bringing a lot of change to Alabama, people who live there still enjoy some of the same things that have always made Alabama a great state. There are still large areas of well-preserved forests and many miles of rivers. Alabama farmers can still make a living on the fertile soil by growing cotton and peanuts and raising livestock. Birmingham remains a major city, not only in producing steel, but also in providing services for all the people of the state. In Huntsville, which has been nicknamed Rocket City, USA, scientists continue to research better equipment for America's space program.

10 KEY DATES IN STATE HISTORY

1. **10,000-7,000 BCE**
Paleo-Indians, believed to be the first humans to live in Alabama, live in temporary, open-air camps that follow migratory animals.

2. **1519**
Spanish explorer Alonso Álvarez de Pineda becomes the first European to see Alabama when he sails into Mobile Bay.

3. **1540**
Hernando de Soto explores Alabama in search of gold. He has a fierce battle with Alabama Natives, resulting in the loss of many men as well as treasure.

4. **December 14, 1819**
Alabama is admitted to the union as the twenty-second state.

5. **January 11, 1861**
Alabama secedes from the Union and joins the Confederate States of America. It provides a significant source of troops and leaders, military material, supplies, food, horses, and mules.

6. **December 1, 1955**
Rosa Parks refuses to give up her seat on a city bus to a white man and is arrested, starting the Montgomery bus boycott.

7. **May 21-25, 1965**
Reverend Dr. Martin Luther King Jr. leads a protest march from Selma to Montgomery. It took three tries for the march to be completed because of opposition from police.

8. **August 29, 2005**
Hurricane Katrina causes widespread damage along the Alabama coast. Sustained winds of 67 mph (108 kmh) were recorded in Mobile.

9. **April 20, 2010**
The *Deepwater Horizon* oil rig explodes. It sinks two days later in the Gulf of Mexico and spills nearly 5 million barrels (596,202,356 liters) of oil in the Gulf.

10. **December 25, 2014**
The movie *Selma* is released, chronicling the civil rights march in 1965.

European architecture was copied in many buildings in Alabama, such as this Greek revival house in Huntsville.

The People

Since the Civil War, the population of Alabama has grown from more than one million to almost five million people. Throughout this time, the state has seen many changes. People from other parts of the country and from around the world have made Alabama their home. Residents have moved from rural areas to urban areas, causing Alabama's cities and suburbs to grow and expand. Today, most Alabamians live in the state's largest cities, which include Birmingham, Mobile, Huntsville, Montgomery, Tuscaloosa, Florence, Anniston, and Gadsden.

The face of Alabama is changing. From 2000 to 2010, Alabama had the third-fastest-growing Hispanic population in the country. Its Hispanic population more than doubled over that decade. Many of the new Hispanics living in Alabama are young. In 2010, 5.9 percent of Alabama's children were Hispanic, which is much higher than the percentage of Hispanics in the total population. A vast majority of the Hispanic and Asian children living in Alabama are citizens of the United States. Also, 30.7 percent of the child population was African American.

The number of foreign-born people living in Alabama has greatly increased in the last twenty-five years. In 1990, only 1.1 percent of the state's population was born outside the

United States. That number had increased to 3.4 percent in 2013. One-third of the foreign-born residents have become citizens of the United States. They can vote, and they pay taxes.

The largest portion of Alabama's population is Caucasian or white. Around 70 percent of the state's residents are of European descent. (This includes people of French, British, and German ancestry, to name just a few.) Some residents are immigrants from those countries, while others may have parents, grandparents, or ancestors from Europe. Several Alabamian families can trace their roots all the way back to European settlers who first came to the region more than one hundred years ago.

Influences from these different European cultures can be found not only in Alabama's people but also in the architecture (the buildings), in cultural events, and in the names of towns and counties throughout the state. For example, Alabama's French culture is reflected in Mobile's celebration of Mardi Gras. The **Creole** culture, which is a mixture of French, African, and Native American cultures, is also present in Alabama. There are Alabamians of Creole descent, and several restaurants in the state serve traditional Creole food.

Place names in Alabama also reflect the state's European ancestry. For example, Cullman County was named after John G. Cullman, a German immigrant who settled in northern Alabama and encouraged other Germans to follow him.

Religion

More than 60 percent of Alabamians consider themselves to be religious. The vast majority of its residents who say they practice a religion are Christian—84 percent. Of those, 61 percent are Protestant, with 37 percent being Baptist. Catholics account for 13 percent. However, a global radio and television broadcasting network carrying programming for Catholics, the Eternal World Television Network, is headquartered in Irondale. Only 1 percent of Alabamians identify themselves as Jewish. Muslims are a growing population as well.

Native Americans

From 10,000 BCE to 7000 BCE, the Paleo-Indians were the first people to live in Alabama. Many of these people did not build permanent homes, but instead traveled with the seasons in search of food. By 1000 BCE, the descendants of these early peoples had lifestyles that were different. These natives started to build permanent settlements. They planted crops and for hunting, used bows and arrows—tools that the earliest of the Paleo-Indians did not have.

The Quilts of Gee's Bend

Southeast of Selma, Gee's Bend is a rural community of about seven hundred. Its quilting tradition goes back to nineteenth-century female slaves. Women made quilts to keep their families warm in unheated shacks with no running water or electricity. They developed a distinctive style and have been exhibited at the Museum of Fine Arts, Houston, the Indianapolis Museum of Art, the Philadelphia Museum of Art, and the Whitney Museum of American Art, among others.

Thousands of years later, native life changed even more. Native groups started working and living close together to improve their hunting success. Organized communities and settlements were developed. In the 1500s, the natives were introduced to European influences. As Europeans came to search for gold or explore the land, many natives were killed by the diseases the Europeans carried or in battles against the newcomers.

When the Europeans returned to the Alabama area in 1700 to try to create permanent settlements, the largest native group they found there was the Muskogee, who were also known as the Creeks. By 1814, the Creeks had signed away most of their land to the US government through many treaties. Most of the Native Americans were then forcibly

Members of the Freemont Missionary Baptist Church belong to the largest Christian denomination in Alabama.

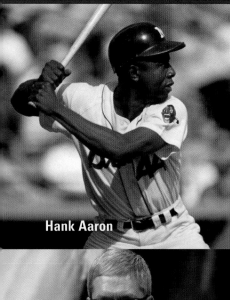

Hank Aaron

1. Hank Aaron

Born in 1934 in Mobile, Henry Louis Aaron began to play semi-pro ball when he was fifteen. "Hammerin' Hank" played twenty-three major league seasons. He is the career leader in runs batted in and total bases, and is second in home runs with 755.

2. Tim Cook

Tim Cook was born in Robertson in 1960. He is the CEO of Apple Inc., the company that produces iPhones, iPads, and Mac computers. Apple Inc. is one of the largest companies in the world.

3. Helen Keller

Helen Keller was born in 1880 in Tuscumbia. Despite losing her sight and hearing at an early age, Keller graduated with honors from Radcliffe College. She spent much of her life helping people with disabilities.

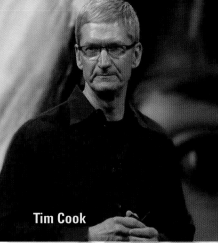

Tim Cook

4. Harper Lee

Nelle Harper Lee was born in 1926 in Monroeville. She is best known for her Pulitzer Prize-winning novel, *To Kill a Mockingbird*, one of the twentieth century's most important books. In 2015 it was announced that her novel *Go Set a Watchman* would be published more than fifty years after it was written.

Harper Lee

5. Jesse Owens

In 1913, Jesse Owens, an African American, was born in Danville. In 1936, he became the fourth American to win three or more gold medals (he won four) in one Olympic Games. He was a sprinter and a long jumper.

6. Rosa Parks

A native of Tuskegee, Rosa Parks is called the mother of the civil rights movement. She refused to give up her seat on a bus to a white person. Her arrest triggered a citywide boycott of Montgomery's buses and protests against segregation all across the United States. Parks died in 2005.

7. Wilson Pickett

Wilson Pickett was a major figure in the development of American soul music, known for his singing and his songwriting. The Prattville native recorded more than fifty hits, including "In the Midnight Hour," "Land of 1,000 Dances," and "Mustang Sally."

8. Condoleezza Rice

Condoleezza Rice was born in Birmingham in 1954. In 2001, she became the first woman to hold the position of national security advisor. In 2005, she became the first African-American woman named US Secretary of State.

9. Octavia Spencer

Born in Montgomery, Alabama, the actress was one of seven children. Her mother, Dellsena, worked as a maid. She won the best supporting actress Academy Award in 2012 for her role as Minny Jackson, a maid in *The Help*.

10. Hank Williams

Legendary singer, songwriter, and guitarist Hiram King "Hank" Williams, Sr. was a country music superstar who died at the age of twenty-nine in 1952. His boyhood home in Georgiana, Alabama, is a museum.

Rosa Parks

Condoleezza Rice

Octavia Spencer

Who Alabamians Are

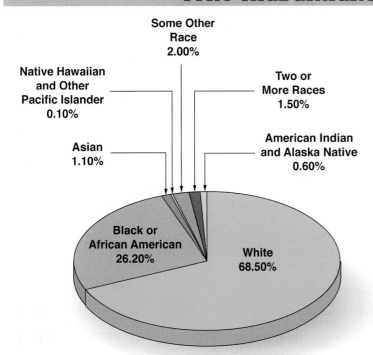

Some Other Race 2.00%

Native Hawaiian and Other Pacific Islander 0.10%

Two or More Races 1.50%

Asian 1.10%

American Indian and Alaska Native 0.60%

Black or African American 26.20%

White 68.50%

**Total Population
4,779,736**

Hispanic or Latino (of any race):
• 185,602 people (3.9%)

Note: The pie chart shows the racial breakdown of the state's population based on the categories used by the US Bureau of the Census. The Census Bureau reports information for Hispanics or Latinos separately, since they may be of any race. Percentages in the pie chart may not add to 100 because of rounding.

Source: US Bureau of the Census, 2010 Census

removed from Alabama. A few Alabamian natives escaped this removal plan. One of these groups is the Poarch Band of Creek Indians.

Today there are about 3,095 members of the Poarch Band of Creeks who still live on their land about 60 miles (97 km) northeast of Mobile. The Poarch Creeks are not the only native people still living in Alabama, though. About 7 percent of the state's total population is of Native American heritage. That means over thirty-three thousand Native Americans make their homes throughout the state. Some live and work in rural communities, while others run businesses or have jobs in the cities. The tribe's Poarch Creek Indian Gaming business manages three gaming facilities in Alabama: the Wind Creek Casino & Hotel in Atmore; Creek Casino Wetumpka; and, Creek Casino Montgomery.

Latinos

Although explorers from Spain were the first Europeans to land on the soil of Alabama, people who are from Spain or have Spanish ancestors make up a very small portion of the population. However, a growing minority are the Latinos. These are residents whose families are from Mexico, Cuba, Puerto Rico, and other countries in Central and South America. Sometimes these residents are also called Hispanic Americans, and they make up about 4 percent of the population.

Hispanics and Latinos are a growing minority in Alabama.

In the past ten years, however, the population of Latino Alabamians has grown more than any other minority group. In 2000, Hispanics made up only 1.7 percent of the state's population. Many Latinos have come to the state to attend the schools, or work and own successful businesses. Several Latino families have been living in Alabama for decades, and there are now Spanish-speaking communities in the state. Most of the new arrivals have come from Mexico, but others have come from Guatemala, Honduras, and other countries in Central and South America. Some experts are predicting that in the future, there will be more Hispanics and Latinos than African Americans living in Alabama.

Asian Americans

About 1.2 percent of Alabama's population is Asian or Asian American. These Alabama citizens or their ancestors have come from Vietnam, Japan, China, Laos, the Philippines, and Cambodia among others. There are some Asian Americans who have lived in Alabama for many generations, while others have arrived only recently. Much of Alabama's Asian-American population is concentrated in Madison, Mobile, Lee, Dale, and Tuscaloosa Counties.

African Americans

In 1721, more than one hundred black slaves aboard the ship the *Africane* were delivered to their Alabama owners. Later, as the cotton crop gained importance to the Alabama economy, more slaves entered the state. By the middle of the nineteenth century, there were almost a half a million slaves living in the state. Not all blacks in Alabama were

The Interstate Mullet Toss

The Interstate Mullet Toss is held the last weekend in April. Participants throw a dead mullet [bait fish] from a 10-foot [3 m] circle in Florida across the state line into Alabama. The winner is the one who tosses the fish the farthest. It is also a fundraiser for local charities.

slaves, though. There was also a small population of freed slaves.

After the Civil War ended, all slaves were freed, but many of them continued to live close to their former owners, who gave them land on which to plant crops. There was a catch to this plan, though. These freed slaves, who were called **sharecroppers**, had to give the landowners a large portion of the food they raised as a form of rent payment for this land. In many instances, they were allowed to keep only enough food to eat, and had none left over to sell for extra money.

One of the main problems for blacks living in the South was segregation, which prevented them from doing many things that white people were allowed to do. Through the efforts of people like Dr. Martin Luther King Jr. and members of such groups as the National Association for the Advancement of Colored People (NAACP), African Americans finally won their civil rights as segregation was made illegal. Coretta Scott King, Dr. King's wife, was born in Marion and graduated from Lincoln High School as **valedictorian**.

Many African Americans still make their homes in Alabama and represent the largest minority in the state, with about 26.5 percent of the population. Like all state residents, African-American Alabamians play an important part in the state's history, economy, and culture. Alabama's racial patterns have distinctly regional dimensions. A broad swath of the northern portion of Alabama is heavily white, as it has been since the founding of the state. Slavery was not as pervasive in that part of the state, and into the twenty-first century the concentration of African Americans is not as heavy in the north as in the south where the plantation experience was more common.

African Americans from Alabama have made many contributions to the country in a variety of professional fields. Condoleezza Rice was the first woman to serve as the country's national security advisor. Mae Jemison was the first African-American female astronaut. Mobile sent some of the first African-American stars to major league baseball. Hank and Tommie Aaron and Willie McCovey went to the big leagues in the 1950s. Hank Aaron broke Babe Ruth's home run record, and he and McCovey were elected to the National Baseball Hall of Fame. Other players from Mobile to reach the Hall of Fame were

People from different backgrounds have come together to make Alabama a better state for everyone.

Ozzie Smith, Billy Williams, and Satchel Paige. Another baseball Hall of Famer, center fielder Willie Mays, was born in Westfield. Leeds native Charles Barkley starred at Auburn University before starting a Hall of Fame career in the National Basketball Association. In the entertainment industry, Nell Carter from Birmingham was an award-winning actress and singer who became famous on television and on Broadway.

No matter where Alabamians come from, one thing many people in the state seem to have in common is a love of music. Alabama is home to hundreds of musicians and musical festivals. Musicians in Alabama are said to be greatly responsible for developing both blues and country music. You can also find zydeco, or Cajun, music from the French Creole people, German polkas, Appalachian fiddling, Hispanic mariachi, American rock and roll, and African-American-inspired jazz and soul. Alabama is also famous for producing music stars such as Nat King Cole, Hank Williams, Lionel Richie, Emmylou Harris, and the Temptations.

Alabama is and has been home to famous people, such as entertainers, politicians, and civil rights leaders, and everyday Alabamians like schoolteachers, bank tellers, and store owners. Alabama residents may be descended from people who settled the land hundreds of years ago, or they may have moved to the state more recently. They may come from different cultures, but Alabamians from a variety of ethnic backgrounds love their state. Some may live in their same hometown all their lives, while others might travel far away. No matter where Alabamians live, no matter how far away some might roam, Alabama will always be where their hearts are.

Alabama Chicken and Egg Festival

Alabama Deep Sea Fishing Rodeo

1. Alabama Chicken and Egg Festival

Over three days in April, the town of Moulton celebrates the state's agricultural roots with the Chicken and Egg Festival. There are music performances, arts and crafts, and, of course, food vendors selling many different kinds of chicken dishes!

2. Alabama Deep Sea Fishing Rodeo

In July, thousands of anglers from across the country fish off the coast of Alabama in the Gulf of Mexico. The 2011 event was, for a time, the largest fishing tournament in the world, according to Guinness World Records.

3. Christmas on the River

Every December, thousands come to Demopolis for the Christmas on the River celebration. The main attraction is the parade of lighted floats that drift down the river at night. The festival includes a children's parade, arts and crafts show, barbeque cook-off, and fireworks.

4. Hank Williams Festival

This tribute to native son Hank Williams includes country music, arts, crafts, and food. The festival is held on the grounds of the Hank Williams Boyhood Home and Museum in Georgiana.

5. The Helen Keller Festival

In June, Tuscumbia honors Helen Keller with a five-day festival. There is a parade, arts and crafts, puppet shows, and sports tournaments. You can also watch a live performance of *The Miracle Worker*, the famous play about Keller's life.

★ ALABAMA ★ ★ ★ ★

★ 6. Mardi Gras in Mobile

Each year, Mobile celebrates Mardi Gras with parades, balls, and parties. The celebration stretches over a two-week period, though some groups begin holding their parties as early as November!

★ 7. National Peanut Festival

Dothan is known as the Peanut Capital of America. In November, the city holds a National Peanut Festival. The celebration lasts for two weeks and has a carnival, fair, parade, and beauty pageant.

★ 8. Rattlesnake Rodeo

Every spring, the town of Opp holds a Rattlesnake Rodeo. There are concerts, beauty pageants, dance contests, and other fun activities. Prizes are given to hunters who catch the most eastern diamondback rattlesnakes. However, some people in the state are trying to get the leaders of Opp to make the festival more wildlife-friendly.

★ 9. Renaissance Faire

In October, Florence puts on a Renaissance Faire to celebrate Europe's culture and history during the Middle Ages, and most fair participants are dressed in traditional clothing. At the fair, you can eat great food, listen to live music performances, and watch knights fight in mock battles.

★ 10. Slocomb Tomato Festival

This family-friendly festival includes live entertainment, parades, music, gospel singing, recipe contests, the Miss Tomato Pageant, and more.

Mardi Gras in Mobile

Rattlesnake Rodeo

Votes in the Alabama Senate can be counted by hand as there are only thirty-five members of that legislative body.

How the Government Works

There are different levels of government in the Heart of Dixie. At the national level, Alabama elects two people to serve in the US Senate and seven people to serve in the House of Representatives. The number of seats each state holds in the House of Representatives is based on its population. Alabama has had seven seats since 1970.

Like other US governors, the governor of Alabama has the power to veto laws passed by the state legislature. Unlike most other states, which require the legislature to garner a two-thirds majority to **override** an executive veto, the Alabama constitution requires only a simple majority within both legislative houses to accomplish this. The governor has a cabinet of officials who run the various government agencies and departments.

Nearly all of Alabama's towns and cities have their own local government. They are not all alike, though. Some cities or towns have mayors and city councils that are elected by the residents. Other cities have a commission or a city manager. Whatever form it takes, local government is responsible for issues that are specific to the town or city. These issues may include land use, school budgets, housing plans and problems, and local law enforcement.

Based on where they are located, Alabama's towns and cities are grouped together into counties. The state has sixty-seven counties. County government is responsible for handling issues that affect multiple towns and cities. Elected county officials include tax

The state capitol is in Montgomery.

assessors, boards of education, county commissioners, and certain judges.

Alabama's state legislature is there to serve Alabamians. In fact, many ideas for bills or laws come from state residents. They consider issues that affect their communities and then point out these issues to their state legislators. For example, the idea to make the blackberry the official state fruit came from young students in Baldwin County. Both the state senate and the state house of representatives passed the bill, and in 2004 the blackberry became Alabama's state fruit.

Alabama's Constitutions

Each state in the Union has its own constitution, which is a legal document that contains a series of laws by which the state is governed. Over the years, the people in Alabama's legislature have written six constitutions.

The first constitution was written when Alabama became a state in 1819. A new constitution replaced it in 1861, around the time of the Civil War. A third was created after the Civil War in 1865, only to be replaced by the fourth constitution in 1868, which was written during Reconstruction. The fifth constitution was written in 1875. And finally, in 1901, the constitution that is still in use today was put into practice.

Alabama's current constitution, with all its amendments, or additions, is the longest constitution in the world. It is 375,000 words long, while most other state constitutions are only about 26,000 words long. Some people in Alabama think the state constitution is too long and too detailed. There are many people who are debating whether Alabama should have a new constitution. These people believe a new constitution would do things such as remove laws that allowed discrimination based on race, and change laws so that more power would be granted to Alabama's cities.

Branches of Government

Executive

The governor, who is the head of the executive branch, is responsible for making sure laws are enforced. He or she can sign a law into practice or veto (reject) a law that the legislature has passed. Alabama's governor is elected and may serve two terms in a row. He or she is eligible to serve again after four years out of office. The executive branch also includes the state's lieutenant governor, secretary of state, attorney general, treasurer, auditor, and commissioner of agriculture industries.

Silly Law

Bear wrestling matches are prohibited in Alabama. A person commits unlawful bear exploitation, a Class B felony, for promoting, being employed at, selling tickets for, surgically altering a bear for, or buying or training a bear for, a bear wrestling match.

Workers remove a Ten Commandments monument from the Alabama Judicial Building on July 19, 2004.

Legislative

The state legislature is called the General Assembly. It is made up of two separate houses called the state senate and the state house of representatives. There are 35 senators and 105 state representatives. Each of these officials is elected into office by Alabama citizens. The legislature is responsible for creating new laws.

Judicial

The judicial branch is headed by the State Supreme Court, which is the highest court in the state. This court is led by a chief justice and eight associate judges. Other lower courts include the court of civil appeals and the court of criminal appeals. The responsibility of the judicial branch is to hear trials and to determine if laws passed by the General Assembly are constitutional.

How a Bill Becomes a Law

According to the Alabama state constitution, no law can be passed unless it first becomes a bill. A bill is a proposed law that has been written out in the proper legal form. There are steps that a bill must go through in order to become a law.

First, the bill is presented to one of the houses of the General Assembly. It is then assigned an official number. The bill is then read to the members of that house on three different occasions. The first time it is read,

Some rooms in the state capitol contain furniture used by the state's original lawmakers.

In Their Own Words

"When I was growing up, my mother and father and family members said, 'Don't get in trouble. Don't get in the way.' I got in trouble. I got in the way. It was necessary trouble."
—John Lewis, congressman and civil rights champion

Term Limits

Term limits for Alabama's governors have changed twice since the original constitution set it at two years in 1819. The term was expanded to four years in the 1901 constitution. An amendment passed in 1968 allows a governor to succeed himself or herself once. This amendment was added to the constitution after George Wallace's first term as governor.

only the title of the bill is mentioned. Then the bill is discussed by a special committee of senators or representatives. For example, if the bill involves a state health issue, then it will be sent to the special committee that focuses on health. If the bill involves education, it will be sent to the special committee for educational issues. It is the committee's job to decide if the bill should be read for the second time in front of all the senators or representatives. Sometimes bills get no further than a committee reading. If the committee approves the bill, though, the second reading is done by mentioning only the title of the bill. It is not until the third reading that the entire bill may be read to all members.

After the third reading, members of the house or senate may debate the bill and the issues it addresses. Changes can be made to the bill. When they are satisfied with the bill, the senators or representatives vote on it. Voting is done differently in the senate than in the house. Since there are only 35 members in the senate, most times the senators' names are called out in alphabetical order, and they give their vote out loud. The process in the house is different because there are 105 representatives, and reading all of the names out loud might take too long. So representatives vote electronically by pushing buttons located on their desks. If enough senators or representatives vote in favor of the bill, it moves to the other house. For example, if the bill was first introduced and approved in the senate, it then goes to the house of representatives.

The bill undergoes mostly the same process in the other half of the General Assembly. The bill is discussed, debated, and possibly changed. If enough officials support the bill, it is passed on to the governor for approval. If the governor approves the bill, he or she signs it into law. The governor can also veto, or reject, the bill. The bill can still become law if enough senators and representatives vote to override the governor.

POLITICAL FIGURES ★
FROM ALABAMA

★ George C. Wallace, governor 1963-1967, 1971-1979, and 1983-1987

Democrat George Corley Wallace Jr. was elected Governor of Alabama three times. Wallace has the third-longest gubernatorial tenure in post-Constitutional US history. His name is synonymous with Southern racial segregation and state's rights. He ran for president four times. He was paralyzed below the waist in a 1972 assassination attempt.

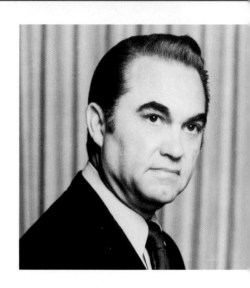

★ John Lewis, US Representative, 1987-

This native of Troy made his name as one of the "Big Six" leaders of the civil rights movement of the 1960s. He marched on Bloody Sunday in Selma, where he suffered a fractured skull while being beaten. He helped register millions of minority voters as director of the Voter Information Project, was elected to congress in Georgia, and has received the Presidential Medal of Freedom.

★ Roy Moore, Chief Justice of Alabama Supreme Court, 2001-2003; 2012-

In 2003, Roy Stewart Moore refused to remove a monument of the Ten Commandments, which he had commissioned, from the Alabama Judicial Building. He did this despite a federal judge's order. On November 13, 2003, the Alabama Court of the Judiciary unanimously removed Moore from his post. He was re-elected in 2012.

ALABAMA
YOU CAN MAKE A DIFFERENCE

★ Contacting Lawmakers

To contact your state and national legislators, visit this website:

www.legislature.state.al.us/

Click on House or Senate in the column at the left of the page. Then click on the Members box. Click on the By ZIP tab and enter your address or your ZIP code. This will give you contact information for all of your elected officials.

You can also find your US senators or congressional representatives at this site:

www.govtrack.us/congress/members/AL

There is a map on the website that shows the geographical areas of each congressional district.

★ Tebow Act on Tenth Try

The Tim Tebow Act, named for the football player with his permission, was first brought to the state legislature in 2005 by a group of citizens who wanted to make sure homeschooled students have equal access to public school sports and extracurricular activities. Legislation was first submitted in 2006 in the Alabama senate and house of representatives, and every year since then. In May 2015, it had passed the house of representatives and was pending before a state senate committee. It would not require schools to guarantee homeschooled students a spot on athletic teams, but give them a chance to try out as long as they met academic and residency requirements. The law would apply beginning in the seventh grade.

Currently, twenty-eight states allow equal access either by law or by permission from their state athletic association. The bill is called the Tim Tebow Act, because the Heisman Trophy winner from the University of Florida was homeschooled and played at Nease High School, near Jacksonville, Florida. Florida passed a bill allowing homeschooled students to play for their local high schools in 1996.

TOUR ENTRANCE

The Battleship Memorial Park in Mobile is among the many sites that draw tourists to Alabama.

Making a Living

Alabama has long been an agricultural state. This means that at one time, most of the state's money came from products raised on farms and plantations. Until the twentieth century, most of Alabama's money came from cotton. Since the time when the boll weevil destroyed many cotton crops, other types of crops have been planted. For instance, Alabama is the third-largest producer of peanuts and peanut products in the United States, behind Georgia and Texas. About 300,000 acres (121,406 ha) of soybeans were harvested in 2011. Other crops that are raised in large amounts include corn, sweet potatoes, watermelons, beans, and peas. Farmers also produce a lot of peaches, pecans, blueberries, and tomatoes.

Not all Alabama crops are used as food. The state also provides plants that go toward the nursery industry. Garden shops throughout the state and around the country sell plants and flowers that have been grown in Alabama. These include azalea bushes, many types of flowers, small trees, and ground cover like ivy.

Crops are not the only way farmers make money. More money in agriculture is made in livestock. In 2013, Alabama farmers owned more than 1.2 million cows. Some of these cows are used on dairy farms, but most are used for food. When the cattle are old enough and big enough, they are shipped to centers in Alabama or neighboring states. Alabama's

Catfish farms are a growing part of Alabama's agricultural economy.

biggest farm product, according to the US Department of Agriculture, is broiler chickens. These small chickens are grown and sold as food and make up about 55 percent of the state's farm income.

A new type of farming in Alabama involves fish. Alabama has about 22,000 acres (8,903 ha) of fish farms. Farmers watch over the fish, making sure they eat a good diet and do not get sick. When the fish are big enough, they are sold to places like restaurants and grocery stores. In Alabama, a lot of catfish are raised in fish farms. Today, Alabama ranks second in the United States in annual catfish sales, and the industry is growing quickly. Some fish farmers also raise ornamental fish. These fish include koi—a large type of carp—and goldfish. People sometimes build ponds in their yards and stock them with koi. Smaller goldfish are usually kept in aquariums in people's homes.

Most of Alabama's fish, however, are still caught in open waters such as the Gulf of Mexico or in Alabama's rivers and reservoirs. There are river-caught catfish, which is one of the most popular fish in Alabama, but there are also saltwater fish such as groupers and snappers that are caught in the Gulf.

Alabama's shrimp and shellfish industry used to provide millions of dollars to the state's economy. Unfortunately, this industry was hit hard by both Hurricane Katrina and the 2010 Gulf oil spill. However, Alabamians are working hard to make this industry profitable once again. In the wake of the oil spill, Alabama's state government has worked with the federal government to repopulate hard-hit oyster beds. New beds are being laid on hundreds of acres of ocean floor. Additionally, Alabama seafood is constantly tested to make sure that it is safe to consume. Some species of fish that had been fished commercially prior to the oil spill have been in decline, but research has not directly connected the spill and the decline.

Mining

Alabama has large deposits of coal and limestone. These are used to make iron and steel, two important products for Alabama's economy. Alabama is the only state that has all the ingredients located within the state to make iron and steel. Alabama is the largest supplier of cast-iron and steel pipe products.

The business of drilling for resources such as oil and natural gas has been expanding in the state over the past twenty years. Today, Alabama ranks fourteenth in the country as a producer of natural gas. Natural gas is used to create energy and heat for homes and businesses.

A natural gas plant rises above a cotton field. These are two of Alabama's most important products.

Manufacturing

The major manufacturing sectors in Alabama are aerospace/defense, automotive, agricultural products/food distribution, metals, forestry products, chemicals, biosciences, and information technology. Much of what is manufactured in the state is exported—in fact, 2012 was a record-breaking year with $19.5 billion in exported goods, an increase of almost 10 percent over 2011.

More than 246,000 Alabamians work in the state's manufacturing industry. Items that are made in Alabama include everything from food and tobacco products to leather,

Aerospace and Flight Research

Automotive

1. Aerospace and Flight Research

Researchers at the Marshall Space Flight Center in Huntsville produced the rocket that propelled the mission for the first landing on the moon and the tools that maintained the Hubble Space Telescope, and designed the International Space Station. It is NASA's largest center.

2. Automotive

Alabama is home to three major automotive assembly plants, three auto engine plants, and nearly four hundred auto suppliers. Alabama's top automakers (Mercedes-Benz, Honda, and Hyundai) produced more than 880,000 vehicles in 2012.

3. Catfish

Catfish farming is one of Alabama's fastest-growing agricultural activities. There are many different species, but the channel catfish is the most common farm-raised type. Most channel catfish weigh between 10 and 20 pounds (4.5–9 kg).

4. Chemicals

The chemical industry contributes nearly $2 billion to Alabama's economy. Chemicals are Alabama's second largest export, producing oxidants, light stabilizers, emissions catalysts, and chlorine. The state's two hundred chemical companies employ more than nine thousand people.

5. Eggs

Chicken eggs are ranked third in Alabama agriculture commodities, accounting for nearly 7 percent of total farming revenue in the state ($288 million). Alabama ranks thirteenth nationally in egg production with more than 9.24 million layers.

Steel

Wood

6. Fishing

Sport fishing is part of the state's tourism industry. Alabamians, as well as people from other places, enjoy fishing in Alabama's rivers, lakes, and streams. Many also take big boats out into the Gulf and spend the day catching big tuna or swordfish.

7. Information Technology

Alabama is becoming a center for information technology (IT). It is home to modeling and simulation technologies, cybersecurity, data centers, defense software development, and emerging media. Its IT industry is expected to add more than 650,000 jobs by 2020.

8. Peanuts

Approximately half the peanuts grown in the US are raised within a 100-mile (161 km) radius of Dothan. Alabama farmers harvested 189,000 acres (76,485 ha) of peanuts, producing 400 million pounds (181,436,948 kg) valued at $118 million.

9. Steel

Alabama's first steel mill opened in 1880. Some of the most decorative steel products from Alabama are wrought iron furniture pieces.

10. Wood Products

About 70 percent of Alabama is forested. Forestry is the state's second largest manufacturing industry, producing almost $13 billion in products annually. There are 650 forest products manufacturing companies employing more than forty-seven thousand people. The state is number one in pulp production nationally.

Recipe for Blackberry Muffins

Blackberries are Alabama's official state fruit.

What You Need

2½ cups (591 milliliters) all-purpose flour

1 tbsp. (14.8 mL) baking powder

½ tsp. (246.5 mL) baking soda

½ tsp. (246.5 mL) salt

½ tsp. (246.5 mL) cinnamon

2 eggs

1 cup (236.6 mL) sour cream

1 tsp. (493 mL) milk

1 cup (236.6 mL) sugar

¼ pound (113.4 grams) melted butter (1 stick)

1 teaspoon (493 mL) vanilla

1½ cups (355 mL) fresh blackberries, cut in half

What To Do

- Preheat oven to 400°F. Grease a twelve muffin pan or line pan with paper muffin cups.
- Whisk the flour, baking powder, baking soda, cinnamon, and salt in a large bowl.
- In a separate bowl, whisk eggs, sour cream, milk, sugar, butter, and vanilla.
- Add the wet mixture to the dry mixture and mix together, just until the dry ingredients are moistened. Add the berries. The batter should not be smooth.
- Divide the batter evenly among the muffin cups. Bake until a toothpick inserted into the middle of one or two of the muffins comes out clean, seventeen to twenty minutes. Let cool for two to three minutes before removing from the pan.

Help For Small Business

The Alabama Small Business Development Center [SMDC] works to help small businesses start or grow. In fiscal year 2010, the SBDC Network served 3,286 small businesses and provided educational training to 7,670 individuals. In that year, 184 new small businesses were started; 519 new jobs were created; and 695 jobs were retained.

paper, and wood products. Chemicals, automobiles, plastics, computers, jewelry, toys, and furniture are also manufactured in Alabama.

But Alabama's traditional industries have gone through significant changes because of the global economy. Many mass-production manufacturers in industries like primary metals and textiles and apparel manufacturing moved their facilities overseas for cheaper labor costs. This trend is expected to continue, with textiles and apparel having the bleakest outlook.

Many companies from other parts of the world, such as Japan and Korea, have built automobile factories in Alabama in recent years. Other large companies in the state manufacture important government-related products such as aerospace equipment and missiles.

There are also large companies in Alabama that process food. This includes human food such as candy and ice cream, but also pet food. Other companies use Alabama's cotton crops to make textiles, or materials for things such as curtains, towels, and clothes.

Much of Alabama is covered by forests. This tugboat is pushing a barge loaded with wood chips up the Tombigbee River.

Alabama's lumber industry is profitable. A large amount of wood is shipped to other parts of the country. Alabama also has factories to process the wood, turning it into useful products like wood chips, furniture, or paper.

The Service Industry

The service industry includes people who provide a service to others. For example, people who work at grocery stores, insurance companies, schools, hospitals, gas stations, hotels, amusement parks, movie theaters, shopping malls, and police and fire departments are all a part of the service industry.

Tourism is a huge part of Alabama's service industry. Alabama's natural beauty attracts tourists from other states and people from all over the world. Its historic sites and busy cities also bring in visitors. Visitors who come to Alabama stay in hotels, eat in restaurants, buy gas, and spend money on entertainment and souvenirs. All of this money helps the state's economy and jobs are created and maintained to support the tourism industry. Today, the tourism industry contributes more than $9.3 billion to Alabama's economy.

Automotive

In 1993, Mercedes-Benz stunned the automotive industry when it announced it was building its first US vehicle-production plant in Vance, Alabama. The announcement came as the state's textile industry was losing thousands of jobs because companies were relocating their facilities to other countries where they could pay workers less and have less regulation.

Mercedes-Benz's decision put Alabama on the radar of other carmakers, and soon Honda, Hyundai, and Toyota opened assembly or engine plants there. ThyssenKrupp followed with a steel plant near Mobile, and then Airbus announced plans to build its first airliner-assembly plant in the United States in Mobile.

Technology

Alabama has worked hard in the last decade or so to make itself attractive to technology companies as a home base. The work has succeeded, as information technology has become a leading industry in the state. The Huntsville/Madison County area of the state alone has more than three hundred international and domestic corporations operating in the region. Tech companies are creating products for modeling and simulation technologies, cybersecurity, and data centers. In addition to research and design, tech companies are manufacturing hardware in Alabama, and the aerospace industry requires a lot of tech support through contractors.

An oil drilling accident in the Gulf of Mexico devastated Alabama's beaches and hurt tourism.

Facing the Future

Alabama was hard hit by the Great Recession that began in 2007. It lost more than 138,000 jobs between 2008 and 2010. But since then the state has been able to rebound on the jobs front, and in rankings of business climate in the United States, Alabama sits in the top third of states. When quality of life and educational opportunities for workers are added in, the ranking declines.

In 2010, as oil gushed into the Gulf of Mexico, many people were worried the oil spill would damage Alabama's beaches beyond repair and destroy the state's fishing and tourism industries. While the oil spill did cause a great deal of damage, the people of Alabama remained resilient. In the years since the oil spill, they have worked hard to restore their beaches and environment and encourage tourists to visit their beautiful state.

The people of Alabama have faced troubled times before, from the Civil War and the unrest of the civil rights movement to natural disasters such as Hurricane Katrina and the tornado that ripped through Tuscaloosa. Much like the Great Depression of the 1930s, the recession of the early 2000s hit Alabama hard. However, Alabamians continue to persevere. They remain hopeful and do their best to help their fellow citizens.

ALABAMA
STATE MAP

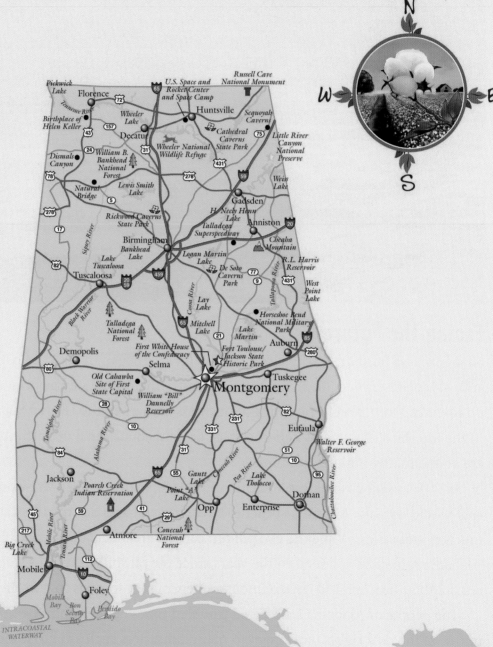

N
W E
S

Pickwick Lake
Florence
Tennessee River
72
65
U.S. Space and Rocket Center and Space Camp
Russell Cave National Monument
Huntsville
Sequoyah Caverns
Birthplace of Helen Keller
43
157
Wheeler Lake
Decatur
24
William B. Bankhead National Forest
31
Wheeler National Wildlife Refuge
Cathedral Caverns State Park
75
Little River Canyon National Preserve
Dismals Canyon
78
Lewis Smith Lake
278
431
Weiss Lake
Natural Bridge
5
59
278
Rickwood Caverns State Park
Gadsden
17
Sipsey River
H. Neely Henn Lake
Anniston
20
82
Birmingham
Bankhead Lake
Talladega Superspeedway
Cheaha Mountain
Logan Martin Lake
77
R.L. Harris Reservoir
9
431
Tuscaloosa
Lake Tuscaloosa
59
459
De Soto Caverns Park
West Point Lake
Black Warrior River
Coosa River
Lay Lake
Tallapoosa River
Talladega National Forest
65
Mitchell Lake
Horseshoe Bend National Military Park
Demopolis
First White House of the Confederacy
21
Lake Martin
Auburn
85
Fort Toulouse/Jackson State Historic Park
280
Selma
Old Cahawba Site of First State Capital
80
Montgomery
Tuskegee
William "Bill" Dannelly Reservoir
28
82
231
Eufaula
10
331
Walter F. George Reservoir
84
31
51
10
95
Jackson
65
55
Gantt Lake
Cheaha River
Pea River
Lake Tholocco
Dothan
Chattahoochee River
Poarch Creek Indian Reservation
Point "A" Lake
41
Opp
Enterprise
45
59
29
Atmore
Conecuh National Forest
217
Big Creek Lake
Mobile River
Tensaw River
112
Mobile
10
Foley
Mobile Bay
Bon Secour Bay
Perdido Bay
Mississippi Sound
INTRACOASTAL WATERWAY

GULF OF MEXICO

miles
0   40

	Interstate Highway		City or Town		Highest Point in the State
	U.S. Highway		Native American Reservation		National Preserve
	State Highway		National Monument		Historic Site
	State Capital		Wildlife Refuge		National Forest

ALABAMA

MAP SKILLS

1. **What is the capital of Alabama?**

2. **How many Interstate highways are in Alabama?**

3. **What is the name of the bay that empties into the Gulf of Mexico?**

4. **How many national forests are in Alabama?**

5. **What city was Helen Keller born near?**

6. **Alabama's first state capital, Old Cahawba, was located outside which city?**

7. **What is the southernmost town in Alabama?**

8. **How many Native American reservations are in Alabama?**

9. **The US Space and Rocket Center is outside what city?**

10. **What river runs along the Alabama-Georgia state line?**

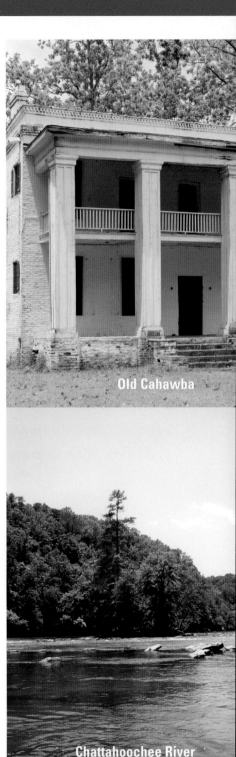

Old Cahawba

Chattahoochee River

10. The Chattahoochee River
9. Huntsville
8. One
7. Foley
6. Selma
5. Florence
4. Four
3. Mobile Bay
2. Six
1. Montgomery

State Flag, Seal, and Song

In 1895, Alabama selected an official state flag. The flag displays a red diagonal cross on a white background. The flag was designed after the Confederate battle flag used during the Civil War.

Alabama's state seal shows a rough map of Alabama, its rivers, and the territories around Alabama. (These territories would later become states.) This seal was originally used as the territorial seal in the 1800s. It was made the official state seal in 1819, but was replaced by a different seal in the late 1860s. In 1939, Alabama's state government decided to use the original seal, and it has been the official seal ever since.

The state song is "Alabama", with words by Julia Strudwick Tutwiler and music by Edna Gockel Gussen. It was adopted in 1931. Tutwiler first wrote it as a poem after returning from studying abroad in Germany. In Germany, patriotism was inspired by music, and she wanted to boost the spirits of her fellow Alabamians.

To hear the tune, visit: **www.youtube.com/watch?v=tn5zHyn3Ujs**

To view the words, visit: **www.50states.com/songs/alabama.htm**

Glossary

boll weevil A beetle that feeds on cotton buds and flowers.

civil rights movement The national effort made by black people and their supporters in the 1950s and 1960s to eliminate segregation and gain equal rights.

Creole A person descended from early French, Spanish, or West Indian settlers of the United States Gulf States who has preserved their speech and culture.

desegregation The elimination of any law or policy that isolates or keeps separate people from different religions or ethnic groups.

Dixie Historical nickname for the states of the southern United States, especially those that joined the Confederacy.

Hurricane Katrina A 2005 hurricane that was the costliest natural disaster, as well as one of the five deadliest hurricanes, in the history of the United States.

livestock Farm animals that are kept for profit.

override An action by a legislature to reject or cancel a decision by an executive.

plateau An area of high ground that is relatively level.

Reconstruction The time period from 1865 to 1877 when the Confederate states returned to the Union.

segregation The enforced separation or isolation of different racial groups in a country, community, or establishment.

sharecropper A tenant on a farm who is allowed by a landowner to use the land in return for a share of the crops produced on the land.

slave A person who is the property of and wholly subject to another.

valedictorian The student who has the highest grades and who gives a speech at the graduation ceremony.

More About Alabama

BOOKS

Gosman, Gillian. *Rosa Parks*. Life Stories. New York: PowerKids Press, 2011.

Levinson, Cynthia. *We've Got a Job: The 1963 Birmingham Children's March*. Atlanta, GA: Peachtree Publishers, 2012.

Lowery, Lynda Blackmon. *Turning 15 on the Road to Freedom: My Story of the Selma Voting Rights March*. New York, NY: Dial Books, 2015.

Rogers, William Warren Sr. and Dr. Leah Rawls Atkins. *Alabama: The History of a Deep South State*. Tuscaloosa: University of Alabama Press, 2010.

WEBSITES

Alabama Department of Archives and History Kids' Page

www.archives.state.al.us/kidspage/kids.html

Alabama History

www.alabama.gov/category/alabama-history

All about Alabama

www.atozkidsstuff.com/alabama.html

Official State of Alabama Homepage

www.alabama.gov

ABOUT THE AUTHORS

Joyce Hart was raised in the South. She is a freelance writer and author who has worked as an educator, an assistant librarian, an editor, and a desktop publisher.

Elissa Bass is a nationally award-winning journalist who has been a reporter and editor for both print and online publications for thirty years. Born and raised in western Massachusetts, she makes her home in Stonington, Connecticut, with her husband, their two children, and their rescued pit bull.

Index

Page numbers in **boldface** are illustrations. Entries in **boldface** are glossary terms.

Index